My Mind In Rhyme, of the Soul

www.myindinrhyme.com

My Mind in Rhyme, of the Soul
Copyright 2015
All rights reserved

First edition published 2015.
Printed in the United States of America.

ISBN: 978-1-4951-2579-9

Book design & layout by Patience, Imagine That!, Missoula, Montana
Cover photo by Bret Posey © 2015

My Mind In Rhyme
of the Soul

Rex Holliday

Dedicated to a woman who has been through most of my life with me, against me,

and stood by me and is weaved in many of my poems.

my wife, Mary Holliday

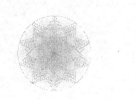

Acknowledgments

I have written in *street* poetry since I was a boy and have had a colorful life to draw on. This form of expression has merely been an escape and therapy for an active mind.

I have had so many encouraging words and help over the last few years from my friends I have made throughout this big world I have been exposed to. My Mind in Rhyme, of the Soul, would never have been accomplished without them. I would like to thank the many who have read my prose and have grown one step closer to eachother in time over the last four years. Besides the "rooters" and acclamations from my many friends, I want the thank Janice Dana Jenkins who helped me start the organization of my work. Mary McWhirter, for her contributions in artwork and for her constant encouragement. Susan Thomas, of *Dramatic Pen Publishing*, without her words and some ideas, I would not have gotten to this point. To Garrett Stanley Photography of Austin, for allowing me access to his photos (you need to look into his work) and to all my Facebook friends for making me believe my work is worth others' reading and helping with art and pictures. Thanks to Christina Anthony for featuring some of my work in *Biker Living Magazine* and the encouragement she has rendered along the way. Finally Patience, who happened to see one of my poems a mutual friend shared on their Facebook wall and loved my work. Thanks to her for saying this has to be published and helping to get it done. I now have the first book (one of three) of the collections of my work.

This is My Mind in Rhyme, of the Soul; to follow will be MMIR, of the Mind and MMIR, of the Heart. Thank you everyone, for your reading of my thoughts and philosophy.

~rx~

My Mind In Rhyme
of the Soul

Contents

My Poetry

I do not expect you to learn the workings of my mind
Please interpret my intentions as created to be kind
I certainly write prose for you to perceive inside yourself
Not leaving your emotions hid away on some back shelf.

If by some great miracle my words to you sound true
Then I have most certainly completed all I set to do
It does give me pleasure to touch you at your soul
Share with you diamonds made from chunks of coal. -rx-

Episcopal Cemetery, Galveston, Texas

Prayer

Oh I love Mother Earth
I was made from her worth
Someday I will return
Don't put me in an Urn.

Just drop me in the dirt
Let me feed flowers shirt
No marker for my place
Let my words be my trace.

Leave behind what I left
In the hearts that I cleft
Return to Mother's womb
Let that be my tomb. ~rx~

Today's Catch

Walking down the dirt road his cuffs rolled up
T-shirt fitted backwards and followed by his pup
Poke pole on his shoulder with a fish on the line
Walking on his bare feet enjoying summertime.

Stopping at the bait store and get a bottled pop
Find a little shade tree where they both could flop
Prop up the poke pole so pup won't get the fish
Taking it home to momma for the dinner dish.

Stretched out on his back looking thru the leaves
Out of white cotton balls are pirates on the reefs
Also seeing elephants coupled with some sheep
As he's loving summertime he drifts off to sleep.

Deep in his dreamland his fantasies are show
His pup gettin hungry starts lickin on his toe
Grabbin up his poke pole still hung with his fish
Singin' to his puppy, *"I'll feed you like ya wish."*

Skippin down the dirt road head for end of day
See tractor run the field smell the new cut hay
Swallows fly in and out of the tractor wheels
Hearin' momma hollerin' he's kickin up heels. ~rx~

Fishing

I'm sitting up on the dock, a dreaming and a wishing
I'm baiting worms on my hook, ready to go fishin'
Distant cast of my line, my bobber hits the surface
Everything that is done is with singleness of purpose.

My eye is on my bob for movement or a ripple
Sitting cocked to one side as though it is a cripple
Layers of the foggy morn dance round the cooling air
Scampish squirrels racing trees with whom I get to share.

Serenity soon goes amiss my bob it goes down under
Jolting current flows throughout from my seat asunder
With graceful ease I jerk the pole the fight it then begins
Stay the water or come out determines who thus wins. ~rx~

Photo courtesy Nola Leyba ©2015

Companion

Sitting in the morning hours the dark not pierced by light
Coffee in my kitchen nook with toast in my dog's sight
Stares at me with such intent her head cocks side to side
Tear a piece to share with her with joy she opens wide.

Seems as tho she's not done her stare returns the same
Now she adds her eyebrows in to play this stupid game
I break another piece as she spins her victory dance
If I think I'd win this game there really is no chance.

She has a few more tricks, lowers her head to look all sad
Or prancing with her front feet to show she is glad
In the end the toast is gone my coffee there to sip
She lays her head by my feet until this day we trip.

So we met the morning sun we walked out in the sand
She would run up ahead come back and lick my hand
She would bark at the waves go running in and out
If there is a better life, well I would surely doubt. ~rx~

Photo courtesy Shirley Gillespie © 2015

Country Style

Sitting in the sunshine walking in the rain
Playing like your goofy acting so insane
Eat some watermelon bar-b-que a while
Living all of summertime in country style.

Fishing on the river swatting at the flies
Strutting down main in front of all the eyes
Anywhere you go walking a country mile
Living all of summertime in country style.

Stop at the tackle shop get a bottled pop
Sitting on porch there wave at local cop
Watch a mother duck with ducklings in file
Waddle down main street in country style.

Listen to the bull frogs singing in the night
Watch sky sparkle with stars as it's light
Listen to quiet no talking it has a smile
Living all of summertime in country style. ~rx~

Photo courtesy of Nola and Robert Leyba

Late Afternoon

Pull on a long sleeve made of denim blue
Sit in my wicker chair rockin back on two
Propped on the porch rail, feet crossed and bare
Listen to the katydids, the squirrels and the hare.

Just as the dusk comes music from the trees
Warms my disposition sends me to my knees
This is the moment of solitude inbred
All the day's trials are far from my head.

Sun singing goodnight hiding in the hills
Moon spreading her light giggling with thrills
Just like clockwork puts my soul at rest
Peace and serenity are tucked in my chest.

Rise from the front porch in to eat the vittles
All of the mountains now seem so very little
Now lay my tired head on my evening dreams
Knowing that tomorrow looks bigger than it seems. ~rx~

Kite Dance

Wind was firm against his kite dancing on the sky
White tattered sheet for a tail with bows to help it fly
With a give on the string the kite would drop in plight
Pull tension back on line to make it climb in flight.

Dancing Tango on the wind gusts pulls it to and fro
Switch to the Samba and Quick-Step puts on a show
Cotton ball clouds and blue sky enhances silhouette
As wind starts dying down dance changed to Minuet.

So it stops takes its bow then falls back in the sand
String rolled up on a stick he picks kite up in hand
Performance of a lifetime it was seen by only one
But on this day with his friend it was a day of fun. ~rx~

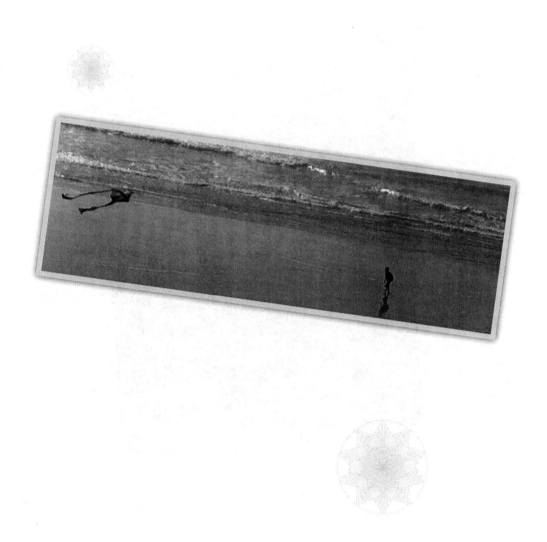

Kids

Sitting on a split rail looking at an anthill
It was doing nothing but just sitting still
Then came Annie with nothing else to do
Kicked at the anthill filling up her shoe.

Jumped down Shirley from the split rail
Tore hole in overalls on a loose nail
Took screaming Annie ran to the house
With water hose gave her quite a dowse.

She cried from ant bites acted pretty mad
Shirley felt terrible that Annie was so sad
Then Momma yelled thru the screen door
"Shirley don't torture little Annie anymore!" ~rx~

Games On

Watching a smart squirrel chatting from the tree
Perched on the limb as he's making fun of me
He had gotten my attention from my easy chair
By running in my garden stealing something there.

Staring with big brown eyes over nut in his jaws
Now he is just chatting like setting out the laws
Then he is laughing as I scream and do a dance
He glides across the limb making quite a prance.

After cursing and throwing I resign he has won
Humbly I turn walking to door I should've run
He throws all of his spoils up against my door
Begging me *"come back out play a little more."* ~rx~

Cowboy Dance

He wore a Cowboy Stetson set down on his eyes
Creased on top of his boots Wranglers fit to size
His finger around a long neck dangled by his side
His eyes on the dance floor to see who could glide.

He walked up to a table with his eye on one of four
Asking that young lady if she'd like to waltz the floor
Offering out his bent arm to escort her out to dance
Looks directly in her eyes she jumps to take a chance.

Gliding 'cross the dance floor together with no faults
Staying to do a two-step country swing and the waltz
Then she said she's tired and needed to get some air
Escorts her to her table she looked back he's not there. ~rx~

Cowboy's Son

He's yodeled with Hank Williams waltzed with Ernie Tubb
Rode the bull at Gilley's and drank longnecks to close the Pub
Fed the stock, mended fences, and birthed calves a time or two
Get up before the sun does, work and play until he's through.

Friday nights for high school football, the Texas National sport
Saturday nights for dancing, almost first, but comes up short
Sunday morning is for sleeping at congregation of the Lord
Merely cuz he's all worn out, it's not about him being bored.

His son will be a cowboy cuz he's taught like tying shoes
He is never pampered 'cause there is so much work to do
Before the time he is born Cowboy songs is what he hears
Momma sings so when he rides, it lasts him through the years. ~rx~

My Dog

Being a man of many words, you're a girl who uses few.
When you're feeling my neglect you find my stuff to chew.
In search of a loving word deep in my eyes you stare.
You love to go on walks with me to show we are a pair.

We spend a life quite simple, together you and me.
Read the paper, chase the ball, see what we can see.
In the morning when I rise you're ready to be fed.
Spend the day at my heels at night it's time for bed. ~rx~

Blessed

Looking to the sunrise peeking on the field
Sending rays of light the grasses are revealed
As the morning brings warmth to the day
All the little rascals come on out to play.

Look intensely for food but stay alert
Not going far from their hole in the dirt
The hawks are flying high up in the sky
Can see for miles with wink of their eye.

Then fawn appears to chew morning cud
Momma looking on if harm hoof will thud
Breathing rather deep filling air in his chest
He's now thinking this morning he is blessed. ~rx~

Photo courtesy Shirley Gillespie © 2015

Nice

Autumn is for the harvest of the summer sun
Like sitting at the table festivities are all done
Colors glare thankfulness, a worship if you will
Falling making bedding, against the winter chill.

Temps are near perfect relief from time of heat
Hear squirrels chatter, woodpeckers keeping beat
It is a time of leisure day planners no longer fill
Days are getting shorter getting ready for the chill. ~rx~

School's Out

Grew during school year, cut jeans into shorts
Wearing nothing else while out building forts
Skin is exposed except band-aides on his cut
Leggings make patches on holes in his butt.

He'll leave at the sunrise come back when sets
If mom's using middle name he'll fly like the jets
Being hot and humid enhances all the fragrance
Cut grass, wild flowers all the animal vagrants.

Washing up for dinner bless food on the plate
Then he'll take a bath after finishing all he ate
Visit with the family then he is sent off to bed
With the feeling that he's sent time way ahead.

Air is window open guarded by wire screens
Lay on sheets in jockeys wishing for his dreams
He'll lay on his back watch shadows on the wall
Sees different creatures and waits for sleep too fall.

Soon he'll hear a 'squito flying buzzing by his ears
Patiently waits till it bites, to end the 'squitos years
Tomorrow start all over and enjoy the summer heat
When autumn is upon him in the class he'll take a seat. ~rx~

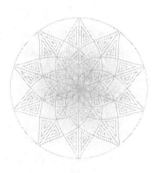

Less Than Perfect

Walk outside in my burb
Stand out front at the curb
'Cross the street children play
Mom brings drinks on a tray.

Walk his dog man gets towed
Right next door grass is mowed
Look to left right up the street
Ice cream truck bringing treats.

As it comes it rings its bell
Seems as though all is well
Walk to sit and unwind
Step in what dog left behind.

Saying things I shouldn't say
Change instead my perfect day
Lesson here if I step in poo
On that foot must wear a shoe. ~rx~

Playtime

I look out my back window to see my grass in frost
A scurrying little squirrel who apparently got lost
Digging in the flower bed where I once had a rose
Many yellow daffodils all sticking out their nose.

He finds a little something he clutches in his hands
Grabs it in his teeth as he looks from where he stands
He runs on over to the tree I'm sure is not his home
Many times I've seen him from limb to limb he'll roam.

Now my entertainment has moved on to other things
Left me here a guessing what else the morning brings
Just about the time that I feel that my gazing's done
I see another squirrel jumping down and on the run. ~rx~

Photo courtesy Nola Leyba © 2015

Grampa

I remember Pap-paw he was sitting in his chair
With his glass of lemonade never showed despair
Always looked at nature as though a part of him
Every little animal and every single limb.

He was like a giant and yet gentle as a lamb
If I had a question the time he did not cram
Everything he said was a lesson that was learned
Turning 'round in my mind like butter being churned.

Now they call me Pap-paw I'm sitting in my chair
But to say I'd be like him certainly isn't fair
He left me such an order of shoes that I should fill
Coupled with his memory if possible then I will. ~rx~

1950 Chevy Truck © 2015

Drive in the Country

Driving through the country in my fifty chevy truck
Put in a little petro with a twenty and a buck
Sitting by my side was my honey dressed to go
Bobbing to the music rockin' from my radio.

Seeing all the stars lighting up the evening sky
Watch as the headlights see the mailbox going by
Feeling as my baby's arm is resting in thru mine
Not caring where we go for we're in the best of time.

Then we hear that oldie song one that we love best
Makes her nod and turn her head on my shoulder rest
It really wouldn't matter if it's raining snow or sleet
There's nothing any better then her heart keeping beat. ~rx~

Photo courtesy Sammi Studebaker © 2015

First Car

On four flat shoes and in high grass
Weathered inside from broken glass
I couldn't see what's in front of me
I could envision what she could be

First I washed her from all soil.
Gave her hours of love and toil
Added parts and made her whole
Cruised the roads, gave her soul

I always knew she felt my love
I kept her pink slip in her glove
If she was with me still today
She'd sell seventy times her pay. ~rx~

Low Ridin'

Under the shade tree waxing up his Merc
Cleaning and shining since he got off work
Shower jeans and T-shirt for his little trip
He is going cruisin' down the center strip.

Wrist drapes the steering other on the shift
When at the red light he has hydraulic lift
Playing on the radio slow dance kind of tune
If the night gets over it happens way too soon.

Waving at his home boys winking at the girls
Smile on their faces showing off their curls
Some hop car to car others with their beau
Enjoy all the company while driving kinda slow. ~rx~

Grows Up Too Fast

Has a CR ball cap turned off to the left
Sounding his loud music loud to go deaf
Coupled to the beat was nod of the head
Standing by his Chevy in fade away red.

Donned in an under shirt from another time
Baggy pants falling off from his behind
One arm tattooed a skull with coin to toss
The other Mother Mary standing at the cross.

Hangs from his right ear ring thru the pierce
Outside the neighborhood looks kind of fierce
At ten plus seven he has much on his plate
He became a daddy on his very first date.

Taking care of family though he himself a kid
Listens to his music grabs a beer pops the lid
Going to wash his Chevy on this sunny afternoon
Hoping that this moment won't go away too soon. ~rx~

Biker

He could feel rumble of his horse between his legs
He just left the Ice House not hanging with the dregs
He was riding in his Levis his do-rag holding tight
A Camel stick non-filter perched tightly with no light.

He sported tats up both arms like the comic strips
He had rings in both ears that whistled on his trips
Wore a shirt that expressed his favorite kind of brew
His Iron Horse hand spit shined looking just like new.

There's nothing like the open road to feel a little free
Feel the air, smell the world, all nature there to see
It was extra special for this Cowboy's end of week
For in the thrill of the ride is the solace that he seeks. ~rx~

Photo courtesy Garrett Stanley Photography © 2015

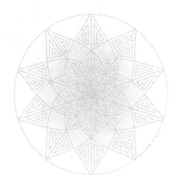

Mary McWhirter © 2015

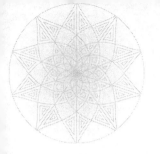

Wind

Life adventure does play with my head
Then wind speaks what needs to be said
Whether gentle breeze or mixed with rain
All words spoken will return me to sane

Dancing with a leaf clinging to the tree
Music played in grasses is symphony
Stirring up the sea to crash to the shore
Bring me comfort I always want more

Messes my hair makes it disarranged
Such is the life the two of us strange
But to feel the wind once never more
Would rip out my soul right to the core. ~rx~

Photo courtesy Garrett Stanley © 2013

Two Up

Riding on a long road in middle of the night
Riding on the Harley and feeling all in flight
Feeling all the wind traveling us thru space
All of life pressures vanish with no trace.

Riding under canopy star light on velvet dark
White lines guide to us to stay within the mark
Trees making faces as outlined by moonlight
Watching as asphalt is penciled by headlight.

Not in need of anything arms clench to my waist
Early kiss 'fore mounting lips linger with the taste
Her warmth pressed against me nose against my skin
As I think about this ride I would rather kiss again. ~rx~

Photo courtesy Garrett Stanley Photography © 2015

Ride

Feeling all the heat on his inner thigh
Wind in his face as highway going by
Push on handles leaning left then right
Rowdy engine music flows with the sight

Shirt with no sleeves jeans on his legs
Completely stretched on highway pegs
Arms on his apes riding thru the miles
Face in contentment shows by his smiles

Heart beats at sixty he travels ninety-five
This is the beauty of feeling all alive
Thinks about stopping doesn't feel it's time
Turning on throttle for miles at double time. ~rx~

Life Rides

May you ride another mile
And do it with a country smile
Take the ride with many friends
Who will go to whatever ends.

Take time to see the sights
As you ride as if in flights
Here the music resonate
Let the life fill your plate.

Then you tell your stories true
To all who didn't ride with you
Then they too may do the ride
Taking all this life in stride.

Build in them stories to tell
How to ride the gates of hell
Builds in you sense of worth
As you ride our heaven on earth. ~rx~

Nice Sunday

Took a little ride with the wind in my hair
Doesn't really matter as I'll ride anywhere.
Enjoying the rumble of engine on my thighs
Riding by myself or with a bunch of guys.

Now I'm kicking back and relaxing like I do
Thought I'd write a ditty, 'bout the day I went thru
Write a couple lines and get a bite to eat
Then I'll hit the road, running with my feet! ~rx~

Haircut Caraway riding 3 Sisters in Texas Hill Country

Philosophy

With a purchased ticket to ride the number nine
Bound up in the distance to run right into time
Is it serendipity or do we have a fate
Destiny to meet the clock no chance of being late?

On this day I choose my life full steam or full bore
So when hitting clock there's no question to implore
And in this moment there's no fears to hold me back
I just feel my happiness by shifting with my tach! ~rx~

Left to right, Jessica Walsh and friend, Jason McGeown, Casey P. Walsh, (standing)Clayton Pulley and friend, Cindy Pierson-Pulley

Family

Riding through the country twenty bikes or more
Stopping at the red light all the engines roar
The light turns our fancy we all move as one
Flows like a dragon slither with morning sun

Giving all the signs that every biker knows
Shifting with the tach lean curves as a show
Find a favorite Ice House Order up a brew
Order from the menu the best bar-b-que

Telling many stories of rides from before
This ride will be a story to tell in legend lore
We all share the love of riding Spirits Road
Hoping that the Spirit does not get our goad.

No matter what befalls us loving what we do
It'll be a story at the Ice House over brew
Then we'll mount our bikes riding in the wind
Riding in the sun like we have committed sin. ~rx~

Republic of Texas Rally

Work and play through this week
Adrenalin rush is what you seek
Laugh and play without sleep
Building memories that you keep.

Work twelve hours on the floor
Then the night life offers more
Bikes take over line the streets
Heart pumps increasing beats.

All the bands play their venue
With full moon giving review
Kickstand bikes parked three deep
Lining up both sides of street.

If this sounds music to your ear
Then I wish that you were here
There's always room for one more
For all those that love to soar. ~rx~

Pooka

Sitting with my demon planning out my day
The only trouble is I never have a say
I know his intention but not how it works
I just know I'll explain away all days quirks.

I don't always see him as he comes and goes
When he makes trouble he follows his nose
If I could ever lose him I would probably be lost
He's been with me forever and boy has it cost.

Sometimes I trick him so events seem real
When it comes out to play I kick up my heel
He can never get me when I'm riding my bike
My Angel is with me as I'm doing what I like.

Sitting with my demons deep down in my core
I'll try to leave him home as I walk out the door
Fire up my engine with my Angel and my bell
Keep me safe through this ride from gates of hell. ~rx~

Photo courtesy Garrett Stanley © 2015

Therapy

Late night stars lighting evening sky
Painting of my dreams of by and by
Sitting in parking lot of a biker bar
Bike on kickstand I'm stretched far.

Think of the times this was all I had
Enjoy the memories even some bad
But on a night with summer breeze
All good memories come with ease.

These are the dreams for by and by
Then start the engine ready to fly
Wind in your hair and the open road
Canopy of stars loosens up your load. ~rx~

Mary McWhirter © 2015

True Love

If you are a not a biker
Two wheels is all you see
Sound of roaring engine
A way thru traffic ease.

But to me she's my lover
My drug for reaching highs
And forsaking no other
I let her between my thighs

In idle she lets a rumble
Vibrating my insides
Wide open she's adrenaline
Touching soul where it abides

Limber in her leaning
Taking curves to the edge
She only does complaining
Left on storage ledge.

She is named as a woman
For a woman she is to me
Riding into the sunset
Forever's my destiny! ~rx~

78

Scattered Mind

I was riding down the center line
Working on my scattered mind
   Running it a red line tach
You think I might be trouble
This might pop your bubble
   Adrenalin just takes me back.

No need to hear the gavel
My soul just wants to travel
   Did God make a bird to fly?
I was not made like others
Though they are my brothers
   In a cage I'll surely die.

While others may be cringin'
At the roaring of my engine
   It is soothing my thinking time
No cell to answer what for
The wind opens my door
   Working on my scattered mind. ~rx~

Jimmy Vaughn

My Soul

Play me a six string or an old banjo
Fire up the fiddle join in the show
Little bit drum added to the sound
All in my head as no one's around.

Rhythm in my body sings to my soul
Melodies dance in my mind on a roll
Music always speaking to why I exist
It can change the world on this I insist.

You can feel it too deep in your core
Do a little count even beat up to four
Add little tapping foot against the ground
Then 'fore you know you'll have a sound. ~rx~

Motley Crue

Blues Night

Sitting in the club and the music jamming loud
With beat of the music movement in the crowd
Lights turned low except colors on the stage
Everyone in the audience was totally engaged.

With each set played music to change moods
People eat it up like a body needing foods
Hungry for the high that's given from the sounds
Dancing with the flavor pleasure thus abounds. ~rx~

Music Playing

Life a bit mundane and you want a little more?
Feel deep inside you the rhythm of your core
Feel the music playing it's living all around
Like when you were little, no stress to be found.

There's song in a friendship, conversations flow
There's still a child inside that you should know
Get your feet a tapping at least inside your head
Just please remember, don't act like your dead

Today is the first day to start your dancing step
Get your body shakin' there's no need to prep
I promise it's inside you, not in another man
You can get the dancing, I promise that you can. ~rx~

Maiden's Song

Sing me a love song
On your mandolin
During the sad parts
Cry with violin

Sing of everlasting
On your harpsichord
Then get it lively
On the ol' washboard

Sing it with the Angels
On a Christmas bell
Sing like you'll keep us
From the depths of Hell

Sing of the ending
On the Saxaphone
Raise from the cold dirt
On the xylophone

Sing me a love song
On your mandolin
During the sad parts
Cry with violin. ~rx~

Wayne A. Milligan, violinist, composer, and guitarist, with his John Juzek Violin,
made by John in Prague, Czechoslovakia circa 1913

John Garr Band

Reggae Beat

You feel it in your bones as it travels to your feet,
Without the music playing you can always feel the beat.
It always keeps you smiling keeps you growing and alive.
You hear it in the Reggae, in the Blues and the Jive.

Cannot keep it going with no music in this place
Keep it going music man filling up our space.

Talkin' with the music and your talkin' with the rhyme
Fingers on the keyboard and your foot's a keepin' time.
Playin' for the people mostly playin' just for you
But sittin' in the audience we get to feel it too.

Cannot keep it going with no music in this place
Keep it going music man filling up our space.

Thank you for your music and Thank you for the beats.
Givin' many people bobbing heads and tapping feet
Certainly with the rhythm we give this day to you.
Playing many years to come baring it anew!

Cannot keep it going with no music in this place
Keep it going music man filling up our space.~rx~

Doo Wop

Standing on the corner
Under the street light
Huddled singing doowop
In the dark of night.

No feel of icy air
Standing 'round the drum
Fire leaping in the dark
While nipping at the rum.

Blending of the voices
Like choir up on high
No feeling of the ghetto
Tonight no one dies.

A capella melodies
Engaged thru our time
Was once just escaping
From death done in rhyme. ~rx~

Delta Blues

A dark black suit and skinny tie
Alto sax with blues engaged
Shades on nose to hide the eye
From one light on center stage.

Fedora is pulled way down tight
All his feelings that were worn
Came from dark not the light
As it flowed out from his horn.

Beauty that the crod did feel
Came from deep inside his gain
In this moment the gift he'd steal
Is a moment that he felt less pain. ~rx~

Salsa

Dress clinged her hip as she walked in the door
Outlining her design taking place on the floor
Her heels started tapping an orchestrated review
Then dancing and spinning with agonizing sinew.

Beat of the Salsa matched the taps of her feet
With the exhausting energy to match any feat
In spite of the speed and flight of the dance
The look in her eyes conveyed a romance.

Ending of the music she gulped down a shot
Sweat runs down her neck showing she is hot
As she leaves quickly on out through the door
I'm remembering the dress when out on the floor. ~rx~

Photo courtesy Garrett Stanley ©2015

Doing What You Like

He sat in the center drinking his ales
Folks all around him hearing his tales
He told of things from distant places
With each event came different faces.

He did it in ballad with whiskey voice
Told of a life he traveled by choice
Played his six-string in simple refrain
Told of his exploits traveled by train.

He sang of the things that he did without
Way that he told it was life with no doubt
His bags and his clothes all showed wear
The dust of the road still clung to his hair.

In spite of the way that he was attired
I noticed his glass is what I admired
Never was empty like stories he'd sing
His listeners of stories did pay everything. ~rx~

Sports

I think it's pretty evident as lines are drawn in sand
For in the middle of the chill, the road to Glory land
The fans pour into stadiums or front rows at the bars
Donning their teams colors and tailgate in their cars.

We began this foreplay with results from last week's blame
Then hype the stats and injury list for outcome of this game
We'll do the same again next week as two teams pack their bags
Then two will play the Championship the winner gets the brags. ~rx~

Baseball

When I think of Baseball, the fences and the parks
All the happy children with their dads yelling barks
Watching as a chess game, decisions moving rooks
Not knowing if the outcome will make the record books.

Smells of pampered grasses, with hot dogs and cold beers
Watching every batter, up with rituals mixed with sneers
Pitcher standing tall at mound, the place where he's a king
Psyching in the batter's mind, searching for the win. ~rx~

Coach

He struts out with purpose at mid line
Looking over faces he has to make shine
Fitted in a dark suit, Stetson to match
Hoping his words in young minds catch.

Then he sounds off with drill sergeant bark
"Some of you kids won't make the mark
If you want more than life you were given
On field of honor you'll learn about livin'.

Just like life you have to stay in bounds
If you step out you'll hear whistle sounds
And like life if you choose your own ways
You'll sit on the bench away from all plays.

You've short term goals just to keep the ball
Long-term goals that make you stand tall
Then a code of honor to stay within the rules
Enforcers on the field with flags as their tools.

You will meet opponents hurdles if you will
You'll find that mountains are really only hills
When the battles over the truth will be known
In defeat or in victory you did it not alone." ~rx~

Photo courtesy Garrett Stanley © 2015

Used To Be

A young man dressed in blue jeans
And buttoned down collared shirt
Watched as a bunch of youngsters
Play some baseball in the dirt.

At home plate the ball was smacked
Went high then bounced at his feet
He threw towards the closest boy
Who stretched to make glove meet.

He heard the boy bark, "you can't throw
your arm missed me by a mile"
He bent and slid his pant leg up
Showed fake leg with a flashing smile.

Then he said he once played ball
Before Army gave green shirt
But he's glad he did that tour
So youngsters can play in dirt. ~rx~

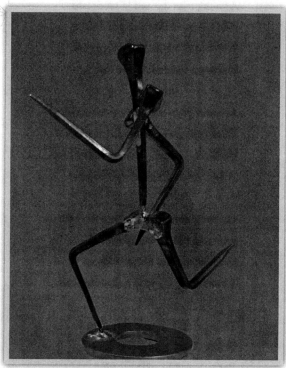

The Runner, artist unknown

Truth of Running

The time is unreasonable to get up out of bed
Bring myself to upright leaving my dreamy head
I bend my back it cries in tune with aching leg
Let's lay here they sing out, "We implore, no we beg."

I dare not look in the mirror at this ungodly hour
How could I show my face scrunched sorely sour
Pull on running clothes damp from sleepy laundry
Make it fit so I feel good has got me in a quandary.

I feel pain as I stretch out as my body's feeling sore
So what's the truth of this run is what you now implore
I walk outside and feel elated as fresh air fills my lungs
This ritual puts me at ease as I climb each mile in rungs.

Running the first half-mile thinking this body will give out
Everything screams at me and gives me all my doubts
After that I feel aligned with the rhythm of my soul
My feet upon the pavement, keeping tune to rock n roll.

Coming to the middle of this mileage I have chose
All living mass of universe within me all then flows
Now at this very moment I am running in the "zone"
Stay there very comfortably until I circle back to home. ~rx~

My Half-Mile

I start every day to make life worthwhile
Every day I go out and run a half a mile
I must say that half-mile is magical at best
For me to get to run it I must run all the rest.

You see for that half-mile cannot stand-alone
It needs the muscles tired so sin will atone
Everything you run today will be of no avail
On that last half a mile your run must impale. ~rx~

Sarah Wind

Awaken

Sipping on my first cup try to get my eyes up
With body screaming *"what's the matter with you"*
Putting on my first shoe think about the avenue
Running in the neighborhood thru the morning dew.

Dress up with a hood pillow felt real good
Going out the front door into the morning light
Now that I'm all done love that I did run
Knowing I am doing what I am doing is right. ~rx~

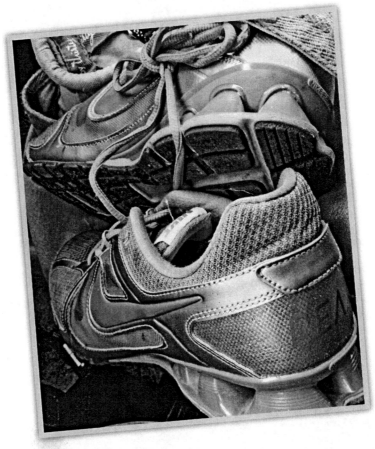

Junk Wars
(Nike™ Challenge)

Pulled my leg up to cross the other knee
Felt for my sock as it's dark and cannot see
Dragging my ass out to do another three
As folks on the other team want to beat me.

Many miles done and the muscles pretty sore
As my shoes are now resting flat on the floor
This is the last day I wasn't doing more
But then the other team evened out the score.

Mighty fine runners push more than you'd guess
As you start running breathing air in your chest
This is where you become the best of the best
Out there running when you have nothing left. ~rx~

Little Things

You wake in the morning thinking this will be your day.

When you go to bed at night you think it's the other way.

But maybe you just missed the joy all along the road.

From the sun up in the sky to the little horny toad

Today I'll check the harbor, to see if my ships come in!

And then I'll check the rainbow for the pot at colors end.

But nestled beneath the sweat and toil it still amazes me.

As sun goes up then goes down the beauty there to see. ~rx~

Night

Could you would you be so kind to reach down in my mind.
Quiet my thoughts oh so deep to rest my mind into sleep!

Thinking through tomorrow's day all the roads to make my way.
Plotting, planning to make it best but right now I need to rest. ~rx~

Tranquillity In My Rest

Thinking in the evening breeze
Soft kind thoughts aimed to please
Tenderly licking all day pains
Left me here with naught but gains.

Back at sunset began the mood
Forgot the ones that acted rude
Moved on in with cool night air
Sound of crickets and frogs to share.

Now I'm bound in my tranquil
Peace is in my mind's fulfill.
I certainly thank the sky expanse.
Tomorrow I have another chance. ~rx~

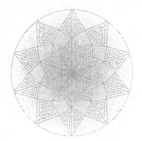

Storm

Illuminated flashing impairs windows of my soul
Ancient sounds of thunder embrace me with it's roll
Resonate vibration of the movement in the air
Oscillates me constantly of elation and despair.

Watching oh so fervently torrent river on the walk
Staring many hours where no others see the gawk
Wishing deep in silence to be sheltered by a rock
For nothing knew of sunshine not an ear or a sock.

Another bolt of brightness came blinding any chance,
Of seeking any refuge from thunders sounding dance.
With each perplexing moment my sanity renounce.
For seriously my essence is filled by every ounce. ~rx~

Life is a Book

I think of little pleasures when younger I mistook.
I spent time alone with me reading from a book.
However I was not alone I traveled seven seas.
Having kings of distant lands bowing before me.

I see the world differently both real and fantasy.
But I notice everything that is put in front of me.
Life is just as a book feel all one goes through.
Conquer demons of one trial or start another new.

Maybe I was captured not knowing how to fend.
Or today I slay a dragon that kept me in his den.
The book has no ending with no burden or no load.
Loving both good and bad I venture down my road. ~rx~

Singing

Sitting in a lawn chair sipping on a beer.
Underneath right eye tattooed with a tear
Then from his left ear hangs a silver ring
To his little daughter he begins to sing

I am your daddy that I will always be
Even when no longer you fit on my knee
You are my treasure attached to my heart
Pity for the man who wants that apart

Walk thru your life the road you will find
Isn't always pretty and isn't always kind
Take what is helpful give back the same
Do what is honest for life is not a game.

I am your daddy that I will always be
Even when no longer you fit on my knee
You are my treasure attached to my heart
Pity for the man who wants that apart ~rx~

Mary McWhirter © 2015

Who?

One to say she's happy and one to say she's sad
One to say she's really good, one to say she's bad
Keeping up her faces seems certainly to be a task
Reaching for her faces to know which is the mask.

She line up all the actors and she plays every part
She becomes the others and yet left behind her heart
Then the mask becomes the existence of her soul
The place where her heart was is nothing but a hole.

In between the changes all her faces gone astray
After the final curtain call she still is in the play
In fact in the dressing room when every mask is off
She'll look at us thru a mask with arrogance and scoff. ~rx~

Restless

On my bed I lay atop
Wait for my mind to stop
Rest now I want to claim
Mind doesn't feel the same.

Displayed is a picture show
Travels where it wants to go
Locks me into endless feats
Keeps me from restful sleep. ~rx~

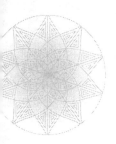

Bandit

Oh yes I am a bandit
I look for your scraps
So you're not looking
I pretend I take naps
Oh yes I am a bandit
I also steal your time
Have you rub my belly
Make faces like a mime
Oh yes I am a bandit
I chew on your shoes
Then I steal your paper
Before you read the news
Oh yes I am a bandit
I also steal your heart
I know you love me
And have from the start. ~rx

Me and my dear friend and bro, Mark Childers

Friends

Sitting with my buddy enjoying summertime
He said, *"I want a Corona with a little lime"*
However we just sit enjoying the afternoon
Knowing this moment will be passing soon.

Sitting under shade tree burning our cigars
Wishing their was someone to fire up guitars
But in the solace of this old shade tree
We are enjoying visiting just him and me. ~rx~

Life Rains

Does it seem there are days it's raining all the time
Never see the light of day the sun will it ever shine
Maybe you might need an umbrella that is plastic
Keeping all the rain at bay feeling like it's magic.

Everywhere that you sit or walk or even play
It appears to be dry just like a sunny day
Oh to own such a thing changes all your mood
Rather than sit inside eating every kind of food.

We shall say it is red dabbled with white dots
That would surely save you when it's raining lots
If you do not believe in the magic of this verse
I guess you'll always be inside where I know it's worse. ~rx

Challenger Park in League City, Texas

Overnight

Using Spanish Moss making me a bed
Also making pillows for my sleepy head
It was done before during the Civil War
Rich got feathers this was for the poor.

It drapes in an elegance blows in the air
Like a pretty woman brushing out her hair
Held in a clump it gives a bedding true
Laying with my dreams till morning dew.

Then at first light I set out on the day
There is no camping fee that I have to pay
Just start the engine warming for the run
Set on the Harley down Highway Fifty-one. ~rx~

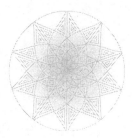

To You

When a friend feels their heart break
Then in my core my soul it will ache
There is nothing that can be fixed
Seems that the world just got nixed.

Some of the lessons I've been taught
On through the obstacles I have fought
That anytime my heart has been tried
The rest of my soul grows and not died.

So to you I will give my hearing ear
And my strong shoulder to catch any tear
Wrap you in my love so you are not alone
Even though we connect only with a phone. ~rx~

You

When I write a post
On a public wall
Maybe it hits home
A triumph or a fall.

I'm glad I can touch
You deep down inside
I don't even know you
Or where you abide.

We all feel the things
Instigating emotions
It makes us all alive
That is the commotion. ~rx~

Celebrate

Death is a celebration of how one lived one's life
Alive is the hardest part living through the strife
When one is gone because of some deep pain
Then we get together and say what a shame.

Might look around and give another a kind word
For in this world what is given is quite absurd
You can be the bird sitting singing the song
So that in another they don't feel life is wrong. ~rx~

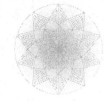

Enjoying

There is that moment in each and every life
That is a treasure even if it comes with strife
Wishes that more often they would come to me
But even once in a lifetime is vast as the sea.

I find in the little things do open up my heart
So that those moments are apparent from the start
Give me those moments to be basking in the sun
Scorch my skin asunder enjoy life for all the fun. ~rx~

 Capture the Mind

From a simple canvas a butterfly can fly
A stroke of a brush it catches every eye
Or with written words you see open sky
If there were not the arts we would surely die ~rx~

Life Is A Story

I try to feel everything each day gives to me.
Things I taste things I hear all there is to see.
In the future to my kids I will tell it all in rhyme.
Certainly I'll start it saying, "Once Upon a Time..."

I have to say that everyone lives an exciting book
But never ever take the time to take a second look.
Some will make a mountain from a tiny bitty hill
Others will say go climb it, so just to get the thrill.

Enjoy each disaster that life can bring your way
Remember you're a story with events from every day.
Books with no tragedy are not read beyond the first
Stirring no emotion the reader never quenches thirst. ~rx~

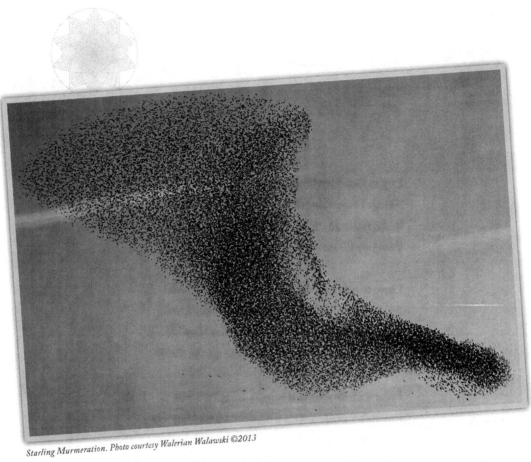

Starling Murmeration. Photo courtesy Walerian Walawski ©2013

California

There's golden rolling hills
Sprinkled with oak trees
California Red Tail Hawks
Gliding on the breeze.

Majestic Cliffs line the shore
Barrier to crashing waves'
People sit watch whales run
This beauty makes us slaves.

Desert land to ride in sand
Mirages dance with heat
Sierra's lined with water falls
Snow capped at their peak.

Beautiful streams and rivers
Form and shaped this land
Over wine fields Starling's fly
Twisted pattern show so grand.

California is just one state
In a Country of beauty land
This one is where I grew up
My path to become a man. ~rx~

Valley

Within the hills of this Valley
Joys and friends I did tally
Drank the grape and came of age
Went to Oz and turned the page

From Box Canyon thru the Knolls
Down to Larwin ran our goals
Every night was party time
Did it all on one thin dime.

Now I'm sixty called a man.
I learned it all in Simi land. ~rx~

Photo courtesy Trudi Fisher Cabrera

Simi Valley

In this Valley rich with history
Was a time of mythical mystery
Kids all came with different tales
Autos, walking and by rails.

Blended magic mixed with time
With Rock music drenched in rhyme
Made us true to each other
You are my sister and my brother.

Now we've been our different roads
Conquered worlds and kissed some toads
But through years what I remember
That we met that first September. ~rx~

Heart Dream

I would give my riches and gold
To live this life and not grow old
To feel the touch of one so dear
To boldly walk so free from fear.

To match the wit of men on high
Watch as arrogance then would die
To see no more excessive greed
To see each child without a need.

I'd sing a song of a life renewed
Secured in hearts as if imbued
That all could feel a love so real
And all sadness of heart to heal.

Yes I'd give my riches and gold
To live this life and not grow old
To feel the touch of one so dear
To boldly walk so free from fear. ~rx~

Pot of Gold

Sliding down the rainbow is really such a thrill.

Grasping colors essence inside you if you will.

Blue is for happiness, harmony from the green.

Yellow for communication yet try not to scream.

Orange makes us social while color purple uplifts.

Red excites our passion and gets us into rifts.

Brown is our roots connects us with our earth.

White represents the clarity we learn since our birth.

So I'll slide the rainbow with colors of time of old.

And when I hit the bottom still might find the gold. ~rx~

With A Gift

Certainly we disagree on what is just and right.
Extract naught from your eye blocked is my own sight.
This may help on life's road arriving at your station.
As my gift I will give my life's delineation.

On the day of your birth you were given life.
To synthesize strength in you you were given strife.
To encourage you to giving naked you were born.
To inculcate humility you toil all that's worn.

You were given your life to lay it down for others.
You were given trials to council all your brothers.
You arrived with nothing to leave here just the same.
So don't count your blessings your posture or your fame.

Everything you need is in sunshine seed and soil.
It will offer sustenance in proportion to your toil.
Do not ask you brother what he should do for you.
You were given strife to arrange your strength anew. ~rx~

Moonshine

Getty up little donkey
Getty up little donkey
You got to get me to the top of this hill
The revenuer's behind me
I hope he don't find me
I gotta get up and disassemble my still.

The last time he caught me
Was the last time he sought me.
Five or six months is the time that I spent.
I expressed my repentance
But the judge still past sentence,
Said that next time it'd be life imprisonment.

I don't see why they holler
I'm just earning a dollar.
They try to catch me and throw me in jail.
It's only corn squeezin's
My customers I'm a pleasin'
Except Sam Barker who looks kind of pale.

Sooo....
Getty up little donkey
Getty up little donkey
You got to get me to the top of this hill
The revenuer's behind me
I hope he don't find me
I gotta get up and disassemble my still. ~rx~

Inward

Looking out my patio door
I'm looking at the sea
As I'm looking I implore
Has it captured me.

I look into its domain
Mighty curling waves
Foam part of its terrain
My soul at crest saves.

Sounds of morning mist
Fall upon my soul
Now added to my list
Close my darkened hole. ~rx~

Photo courtesy Garrett Stanley © 2015

Church

The road looks like a river in the Texas heat
I think the tar is melting the ride is still sweet
Running wide open to dry baptism in sweat
From you hair to your boots everything is wet.

Take hands off the grips to play the air guitar
Fingers sling the sweat that moment I'm a star
Grasping on the throttle to lean into next curve
See the hole in road rotate the lean to swerve.

I am baptized from the heat the fire of the road
With the wind in my hair releases every load
When it rains it cools down washes out my sin
I can ride into the night for stars they are my kin. ~rx~

I'm Ready for Bed Because

Eradicating my contemplating of useless things despair

Organizing and minimizing thoughts I need not share

So I think I'm on the brink of sweeping with my broom

I ascertain that my brain is clean from room to room

So certainly as the time must be not be confused

For it's at rest and at its best not to be abused. ~rx~

Mirrored

Whimsically wondering thoughts ensue
Daintily daring in conversing anew
Cautiously choosing words which to use
Sharing staring these thoughts I do muse.

Thoughtfully trusting the paths I do walk
Metaphorically mounting my mind that I stalk
Bountifully baring just parts of my soul
Gallantly guarding to not take its toll.

Eventually editing the language that's said
Beautifully bouncing all that's been read
Fortunately faring as to all that will sell
Posthumously preparing thoughts in well. ~rx~

Cold Days

I am buried deeply with blankets for my clothes
I can feel the icy cold come through on my toes
If I move a quarter inch the sheet gives icy blast
That is why I am stuck right here molded in my cast.

Alarm is quite annoying, piercing screams in the dark
Balancing the pro and con it's sounding like a Lark
I'm stuck in this dilemma 'cause I have to go to work
That can't be accomplished lest I make the coffee perk.

Then with firm conviction I dash to jump in jeans
I twist and turn, do my dance and let out little screams
When I'm almost ready I hear the church bells chime
I realize then it's Sunday, God I pray for summertime. ~rx~

Pelicans on Ft Bayou, Oak Glen Marina, Pelicans, photo by Terri Nyers Downs © 2015

Florida Fishing

Little pterodactyls in the sky
Watching Pelicans as they fly
Scoping surface of waters edge
A days fish is what they pledge.

Wings stroke strong as he climbs
Riding currents like ancient times
Diving deep easily get his prey
With strong beak he makes fillet

So much more than a fishing pole
While casting line at a fishing hole
Free in wind and gliding the sky
When pot luck meets the eye. ~rx~

End Words

Words just paint a picture of the wandering of mind
If not painted carefully they will be taken as unkind
Paint silhouettes of masters on canvass of your soul
When words are spoken they won't sound very cold

Choose words carefully say what springs a thought
It doesn't mean anything if in others nothing's caught
One must only plant the seed and others make it grow
That will make words you use bigger than you know. ~rx~

Index: Photos and Illustrations (all photos and illustrations used by permission)

~rx~